T0011180

TOUCHDOWNS
and
TAILGATES
Behind the Scenes
of Game Day Football

by Martin Driscoll

CAPSTONE PRESS
a capstone imprint

Published by Spark, an imprint of Capstone
1710 Roe Crest Drive, North Mankato, Minnesota 56003
capstonepub.com

Library of Congress Cataloging-in-Publication Data is available on the Library of Congress website.

ISBN: 9781669003274 (hardcover)
ISBN: 9781669040491 (paperback)
ISBN: 9781669003236 (ebook PDF)

Summary: Think pro football begins with the opening kickoff? Think again! In this Sports Illustrated Kids book, go behind the scenes of a typical game day in professional football—from pregame tailgating and prepping the pigskins to halftime shows and postgame interviews. This fast-paced, fact-filled book will give football fans of all ages a fresh new perspective on America's Game.

Editorial Credits
Editor: Donald Lemke; Designer: Tracy Davies; Media Researcher: Svetlana Zhurkin; Production Specialist: Katy LaVigne

Image Credits
Alamy: Cal Sport Media/Charles Baus, 13, UPI/John Angelillo, 11; Associated Press: Ben Liebenberg, 8, James D. Smith, 19, Jim Mahoney, 7, Logan Bowles, 21; Getty Images: Bryan M. Bennet, 14, David Eulitt, 26, Dziurek, cover (bottom middle), Frederick Breedon, 25, Jamie Squire, 9, John Grieshop, 17, Julio Aguilar, 5, Katelyn Mulcahy, 16, Kevin Hoffman, 15, Ronald Martinez, 24, San Francisco 49ers/Michael Zagaris, 18, 23, 27, Stacy Revere, 4, The Boston Globe/Jim Davis, 6, Thomas Barwick, cover (bottom right), Todd Kirkland, 12, Tom Pennington, 10; Newscom: Icon Sportswire/Kiyoshi Mio, 22; Shutterstock: Elena Veselova, 29 (back), M. Budniak, 29 (bottom), Mtsaride, cover (top right), 1, 29 (inset, bottom), Ron Dale (background), cover, back cover, Sean Locke Photography, cover (bottom left), winui, cover (top); Sports Illustrated: Erick W. Rasco, 20

TABLE OF CONTENTS

Words in **bold** are in the glossary.

GAME DAY FUN

Nothing beats a football game on a fall day. And nothing beats the National Football League (NFL) for excitement. The best football teams in the world compete in the NFL.

Fans cheer at Raymond James Stadium in Tampa, Florida.

Thousands of fans fill NFL **stadiums** every week. Millions more fans watch the action on TV. They root for their favorite teams.

GETTING READY

The stadium gets busy before the game begins. The grounds crew prepares the field. They use white paint to make the yard lines on the field. They paint the **end zones** with the home team's colors.

A grounds crew paints the logo of the New England Patriots on the field.

The Miami Dolphins grounds crew mows the field prior to a game.

There are 32 teams in the NFL. Sixteen NFL stadiums have real grass. The others have **artificial turf**.

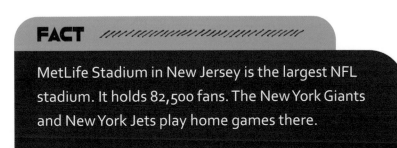

FACT //

MetLife Stadium in New Jersey is the largest NFL stadium. It holds 82,500 fans. The New York Giants and New York Jets play home games there.

Players get to the stadium a few hours before game time. They head to the locker room. They put on their pads and uniforms.

The Cincinnati Bengals locker room

Kansas City Chiefs quarterback Patrick Mahomes warming up

Some stretch and jog to warm up for the game. Other players wait for help from team trainers. The trainers tape up ankles, knees, and wrists. This helps **prevent** injuries.

KICKOFF TIME

Game time is near. The stadium is packed. The home team waits in a tunnel between the locker room and the field.

Cheerleaders line up on the field. They perform a dance **routine**. The crowd roars as its team sprints out of the tunnel.

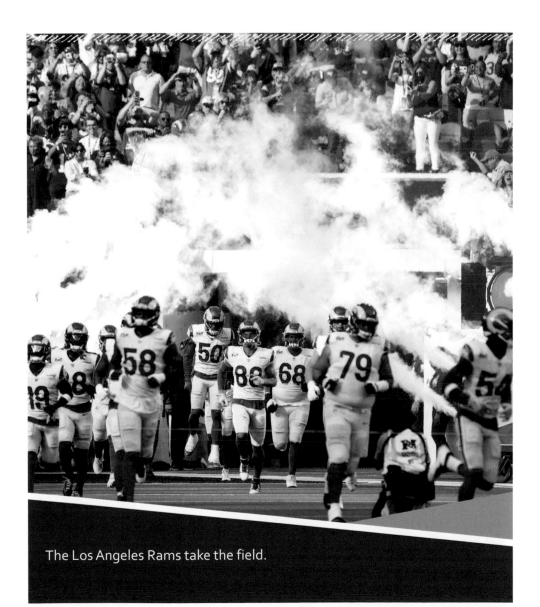

The Los Angeles Rams take the field.

The game begins with a coin toss. Captains from both teams meet at **midfield**. The referee or a special guest tosses the coin.

A captain from the visiting team must call "heads" or "tails." If he guesses right, he chooses which team gets the ball first.

Tennis legend Billie Jean King tosses the coin before the Super Bowl game in 2022.

The referee is one of seven officials on the field for NFL games.

13

SPEED AND SKILL

Football is a game of speed, skill, and strength. A long pass takes all of those things. The wide receiver must be quick to get open. The quarterback must be skilled and strong to make a perfect throw.

Buffalo Bills wide receiver Stefon Diggs dives for a touchdown.

FACT //

In 2021, Browns quarterback Baker Mayfield threw a touchdown pass that set an NFL record. The ball was in the air for over 66 yards. No player had ever completed a pass that traveled so far in the air.

Players on defense also must have speed, strength, and skill. Linemen are often the biggest players on defense. Linebackers must be quick to catch **ballcarriers**.

Los Angeles Rams Jalen Ramsey tackles an Arizona Cardinals player.

Denver Broncos defensive player Justin Simmons

They also must be strong enough to tackle runners. Defensive backs must be fast enough to keep up with receivers. They also need great skills to break up pass plays.

Each NFL team has 46 players in uniform for every game. Only 11 of them are on the field. The rest of them wait on the sideline.

The sideline is a busy place. Players use tablet computers to look at replays from the game. This helps them understand the **strategy** of the other team.

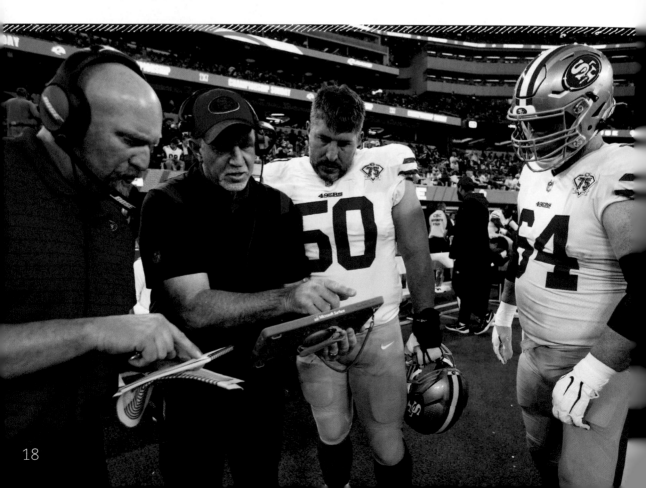

Assistant coaches give instructions to players. Other staff members help players with injuries and equipment.

A lot happens at NFL games that fans never see. In the control room, a team of workers puts on a show for the crowd. These people run the lights, video, and music in the stadium.

They decide when to play loud music to pump up the crowd. They also decide when to show replays on the big screen.

CRUNCH TIME

Halftime gives the players a chance to rest. They head back to the locker room. They might grab an energy bar to eat. They might visit the trainer to have a wrist or ankle taped.

The coaching staff is busy at halftime.

The head coach meets with his assistants.

Then the head coach speaks to the team.

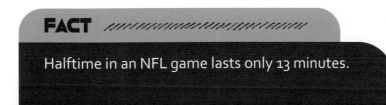

FACT

Halftime in an NFL game lasts only 13 minutes.

Imagine you are at an NFL game. The score is close in the fourth quarter. A field goal could give your team the win. The placekicker comes onto the field.

Los Angeles Rams kicker Matt Gay (8)

Minnesota Vikings kicker Daniel Carlson attempts to kick a field goal.

Most NFL players are big and powerful. Often the kicker is the smallest player on the field. But he has great skill. He can kick a football a long way.

FACT

NFL goalposts must be 18.5 feet (5.6 meters) apart. The crossbar must stand 10 feet (3.05 m) off the ground. The goalposts must be 35 feet (10.7 m) tall.

Football is a tough sport. Pro players battle for 60 minutes in each game. When time runs out, the fight is over. The players shake hands.

Back in the locker room, the winners can celebrate. The losers may discuss what went wrong. Soon they will all move on. The next game day is only a week away.

PLAN YOUR GAME DAY

At many NFL stadiums, fans have tailgate parties in the parking lot. They show up early. They bring lawn chairs and charcoal grills. And they have fun with family and friends.

You can have a tailgate party in your backyard.

- Invite some friends over to watch the game.
- Ask your parents to grill burgers and hot dogs.
- Have chips and soft drinks ready to share.
- Set up for beanbag toss and other yard games.
- Head inside at game time and watch the action.
- At halftime, get outdoors for a quick game of touch football.

GLOSSARY

artificial turf (art-uh-FISH-uhl TURF)—a human-made material used in place of natural grass

ballcarrier (BAHL-kayr-ee-ur)—a football player who carries the ball on offense

end zone (END ZOHN)—the area beyond the goal line at each end of a football field

midfield (MID-feeld)—the portion of a playing field that is midway between goals

prevent (pri-VENT)—to keep from happening

routine (roo-TEEN)—a part that is carefully worked out so it can be repeated often

stadium (STAY-dee-uhm)—a large, usually roofless, building with rows of seats for spectators at modern sports events

strategy (STRAT-uh-jee)—a careful plan used in a game or other competition

READ MORE

Nelson, Robin. *The Story of a Football: It Starts with Leather.* Minneapolis: Lerner, 2022.

Omoth, Tyler. *Football Fun*. North Mankato, MN: Capstone, 2021.

Storden, Thom. *Big-Time Football Records*. North Mankato, MN: Capstone, 2022.

INTERNET SITES

NFL Play Football
playfootball.nfl.com

Pro Football Hall of Fame
profootballhof.com

Sports Illustrated Kids: Football
sikids.com/football

INDEX

ABOUT THE AUTHOR

Martin Driscoll is a former newspaper reporter and longtime editor of children's books. He is also the author of several sports books for children, including biographies of legendary stars of boxing, baseball, and basketball. Driscoll lives in southern Minnesota with his wife and two children.